Cumbria Libraries

3 8003 04476 2979

KU-615-340

This book is on loan from
Library Services for Schools
www.cumbria.gov.uk/
libraries/schoolslibserv

Cumbria
County Council

Systems of Government

COMMUNISM

Sean Connolly

W
FRANKLIN WATTS
LONDON•SYDNEY

 An Appleseed Editions book

First published in 2013 by Franklin Watts
338 Euston Road, London NW1 3BH

Franklin Watts Australia
Hachette Children's Books
Level 17/207 Kent St, Sydney, NSW 2000

© 2012 Appleseed Editions

Created by Appleseed Editions Ltd,
Well House, Friars Hill, Guestling,
East Sussex TN35 4ET

Designed by Hel James
Edited by Mary-Jane Wilkins
Picture research by Su Alexander

LIBRARY SERVICES FOR SCHOOLS	
38003044762979	
Bertrams	01/08/2013
321.92	£12.99
LSS	

All rights reserved. No part of this publication may be reproduced, stored
in a retrieval system or transmitted in any form or by any means, electronic, mechanical,
photocopying, recording or otherwise, without prior permission of the publisher.

ISBN 978 1 4451 0986 2

Dewey Classification 321.9'2

A CIP catalogue for this book is available from the British Library.

Picture credits
page 5 Thinkstock; 7 Library of Congress/Getty Images; 8 English School/Getty Images;
10 & 13 AFP/Getty Images; 14 Photos.com/Thinkstock; 17 Gamma-Keystone via Getty
Images; 19 AFP/Getty Images; 20, 22 & 24 Getty Images; w25 Kojoku/Shutterstock;
26 & 29 Getty Images; 30 Igor Golovniov/Shutterstock; 31 Kamira/Shutterstock;
33 Time & Life Pictures/Getty Images; 36 NY Daily News via Getty Images;
38 & 39 AFP/Getty Images; 40 Phshnyy Maxim Vjacheslavovich/Shutterstock;
42 Gamma-Rapho via Getty Images; 45 AFP/Getty Images

Printed in Malaysia

Franklin Watts is a division of Hachette Children's Books,
an Hachette UK company.
www.hachette.co.uk

Contents

What is communism?

Imagine waking up every morning and wondering whether the world will be blown away that day. Maybe the disaster would be the result of a world leader mishearing some information on the telephone. Or perhaps a trigger-happy general or air force pilot had pressed a button and sent a missile shooting across the world.

Many people – young and old – suffered constant anxiety of this kind between the years 1945 and 1990. That forty-five year period is often called the **Cold War** because the world was fiercely divided and seemed to be constantly on the point of going to war. On one side of the divide were the countries of **western** Europe and North America, plus other countries that shared their political values. These values include the right to elect political leaders, to own property and businesses and to travel freely both inside one's own country and beyond.

On the other side were ranged the **Soviet Union**, the countries of eastern Europe, China and other nations with communist governments. Their political system – which gives the government massive power and allows citizens less individual choice – was at odds with western ideas of freedom.

Crisis averted

Each side distrusted and feared the other, so much so that many people feared that a third world war might break out at any time. Both sides had armed themselves with destructive nuclear weapons, and a disagreement about types of government could have led to catastrophe. Most people in the west breathed a sigh of relief when country after country abandoned communism during the late 1980s and early 1990s. But several countries – notably the world's largest country, China – have remained communist.

This book examines how communist governments worked, and continue to work. Is communism really a fairer system, as its

TIMELINE... TIMELINE... TIMELINE... TIMELINE... TIMELINE... TIMELINE

CE **1848**   **Karl Marx and Friedrich Engels publish the *Communist Manifesto***

supporters claim? Was it doomed to failure? Can it change to meet the challenges of the modern world? The first two questions look set to divide public opinion for many years to come. The last is more likely to be answered in the near future. Maybe the world will see a new system emerging, adopting some communist elements. On the other hand, it could be that only history books will deal with the subject of communism in future.

The national flag hangs down over rooftop chicken coops in Cuba, one of the last remaining communist countries in the world.

A permanent revolution?

Most people, wherever they live in the world, believe that **democracy** involves holding free elections to choose (or to vote out) political leaders. One of the last remaining communist countries is North Korea; its official title is the Democratic People's Republic of Korea – yet the country is not ruled in a democratic manner. Many communist countries, both past and present, include the word 'democratic' in their name, even though they deny their citizens many of the rights that people expect in democracies.

'**Republic**' is another word which crops up in the name of many communist countries (such as North Korea). Again, a communist republic appears to be very different from one which is not communist. Like democracies, most republics rely on elected leaders to represent the wishes of the people. Communist governments also depend on the decisions of a relatively small group of political leaders, whose actions are intended to benefit the wider population (just as they do in other countries). The main difference is that the small group who lead the government have not been elected by the people whose lives they govern.

Following a pattern

What sets communism so far apart from other forms of government? Much of the answer comes from the communist belief that countries naturally move on from one type of government to another over history (see panel on page 9). Great changes come about – according to this view – not through the efforts of individuals but through the actions of large groups of people (known as **classes**).

TIMELINE... TIMELINE... TIMELINE... TIMELINE... TIMELINE... TIMELINE.

1905   The first soviet (council of workers) set up in St Petersburg, Russia

VOICE OF THE PEOPLE

THE COMMUNIST GOAL

Leon Trotsky (1879–1940) was one of the architects of the Russian Revolution. He believed that people would become happy once they had followed a historic struggle and true communism was achieved. In 1924 he expressed his optimism about a communist society: 'Man will become immeasurably stronger, wiser, and subtler; his body will become more harmonious, his movements more rhythmic, his voice more musical. The forms of life will become dynamically dramatic. The average human type will rise to the heights of an Aristotle, a Goethe, or a Marx. And above these heights, new peaks will rise.'

Leon Trotsky (shown here in Paris) helped to lead the Russian Revolution, but was forced to leave the Soviet Union in 1929 by Josef Stalin, who feared Trotsky as a rival for the leadership. Trotsky was eventually murdered in Mexico in 1940 by a Soviet agent.

TIMELINE... TIMELINE... TIMELINE... TIMELINE... TIMELINE... TIMELINE...

1912   Lenin forms the Bolsheviks into a separate party, with himself as leader

Communists argue that classes of people sweep aside an older style of government and replace it with a type of government that suits their needs better. Such a shift involves a wide-ranging upheaval, or revolution. Nearly every communist **regime** in history came to power through some sort of revolution.

This line of thinking leads to a problem that most communist systems have faced: will events eventually produce a revolution that will topple communism? Or – as Leon Trotsky and other Russian communists argued in the 1920s – will the world face a 'permanent revolution' in which true communists continue to struggle against those who prefer the old ways?

*A late fifteenth-century illustration depicts a busy farming scene in feudal Europe, with **serfs** hard at work on a lord's estate.*

TIMELINE... TIMELINE... TIMELINE... TIMELINE... TIMELINE... TIMELINE...

1917　Lenin leads the Bolshevik Revolution, establishing communism in Russia
1917–21　Civil war in Russia; opponents of communism try to overthrow government

COMMUNIST STAGES OF HISTORY

Just as religious people turn to sacred books such as the Bible and the Koran for answers, communists study the works of German political philosopher Karl Marx (1818–83) for inspiration. Marx's book *The Communist Manifesto* introduced the term communism to the world in 1848 and over the years he developed his theory of how human society advances through history.

Marx identified six historical stages, described below. Note that even governments we consider to be communist describe themselves as socialist, and that the final stage of communism remains a goal.

Primitive communism

This stage represents the earliest form of human society, in which hunter-gatherers live together with no leadership and no private property.

Slave society

Two classes appear at this stage – slave-owners and slaves. Land is farmed to provide food for a growing population. Democracies and republics are formed, along with **empires**.

Feudalism

In this stage individual nations dominate, with clear-cut classes ranging from the ruling monarch and upper classes which pass down wealth through the generations at the top, down to serfs, who worked on a lord's land.

Capitalism

Merchants who have grown rich (or amassed capital) own the means of production, such as factories, and pay workers to produce goods in them. Elected governments become common.

Socialism

By this stage workers have gained more power and – most importantly – control the means of production rather than factory owners. Central government loses power as people take greater control of their own lives.

Communism

The final stage that Marx described is an advanced form of socialism: everyone shares all property and there is no organized government.

Seizing control

NHIỆT LIỆT CHÀO MỪNG
ĐẠI HỘI ĐẠI BIỂU TOÀN QUỐC
LẦN THỨ X CỦA ĐẢNG

When the coalition of Conservatives and Liberal Democrats assumed power in the UK in 2010, they did so knowing that between them they had enough seats in Parliament to form a government. A British general election usually provides a **mandate** for one of the parties to form a government by winning enough seats to outvote the opposition in Parliament.

TIMELINE... TIMELINE... TIMELINE... TIMELINE... TIMELINE... TIMELINE.

1919–20   German Communist Party leads uprising in Germany; soldiers crush revolt

Young people gaze at a bright future in a huge poster in Vietnam. Behind them is the smiling face of Ho Chi Minh, who set the country on the path towards communism in the 1940s.

Whether a single party achieves a mandate, or two parties combine to form a **coalition** government, the system generally reflects the views of the voters. The voters also have the final say in choosing their leaders in other forms of democracy, such as those in the United States, Germany and France.

Different routes

Communist systems are different. Communists believe that social change comes about not through elections, but through mass movements that sweep away old systems of government (see pages 6–9). They also believe that the electoral system followed by people in Britain, the United States and elsewhere is simply a way of keeping working people in their place.

Communist thinkers would see little difference between the Labour and Conservative parties in the UK, or the Democrat and Republican parties in the United States. They believe that political parties exist to keep capitalists (the people who have money) in power. Improving working people's lives here and there, for example by paying better wages or allowing longer holidays, is simply a way of stopping those people from overthrowing the system. Communists describe democracies such as those in Britain and the United States as **bourgeois**, which comes from a French word referring to property-owning townspeople.

Some communist parties in Europe and South America have been prepared to join in bourgeois elections rather than threaten the system with violent upheaval (see pages 26–30). Others have followed a more traditionally **Marxist** route to revolution – this is how communism took root in Russia, China and Cuba. Major communist powers, such as the Soviet Union and China, provided aid and weapons to anti-colonial movements in Africa and Asia in the decades after the **Second World War**. Many of these countries adopted communist governments when they gained independence.

TIMELINE... TIMELINE... TIMELINE... TIMELINE... TIMELINE... TIMELINE...

1921   Lenin's New Economic Policy reverses communist policy; allows **peasants** to sell surplus food

DIFFERING ACCOUNTS

What people consider to be history often reflects the personal views of those who witnessed great historical events. The following are two accounts of the storming of the Winter Palace by the Bolsheviks (communists) on 25 October 1917. The ruler, the **tsar**, had been **deposed** earlier that year, but Russia's **provisional government** had based itself in the palace, keeping it intact. Hundreds of Bolsheviks flooded into the palace and it became a symbol of the communist victory.

How people behaved inside the palace is hard for us to judge. Here is an eyewitness account written by a reporter from the *Guardian* newspaper: 'The Palace was pillaged and devastated from top to bottom by the Bolshevik armed mob, as though by a horde of barbarians. All the State papers were destroyed. Priceless pictures were ripped from their frames... Several hundred carefully packed boxes of rare plate and china... were broken open and the contents smashed or carried off. The library of Alexander III... was forced open and ransacked, books and manuscripts burnt and destroyed.' from *Guardian Century,* http://century.guardian. co.uk/1910-1919/Story/0,126504,00.html

A second account is by John Reed, a young American reporter from a privileged background who was drawn to the the Russian Revolution in 1917: 'One man went strutting around with a bronze clock perched on his shoulder; another found a plume of ostrich feathers, which he stuck in his hat. The looting was just beginning when somebody cried, "**Comrades**! Don't touch anything! Don't take anything! This is the property of the People!" Immediately twenty voices were crying, "Stop! Put everything back! Don't take anything! Property of the People!" Many hands dragged the spoilers down. **Damask** and tapestry were snatched from the arms of those who had them; two men took away the bronze clock. Roughly and hastily the things were crammed back in their cases, and self-appointed sentinels stood guard. It was all utterly spontaneous. Through corridors and up staircases the cry could be heard growing fainter and fainter in the distance, "Revolutionary discipline! Property of the People".' from *The Bolsheviks Storm the Winter Palace*, 1917 EyeWitness to History, www.eyewitnesstohistory.com 2006

1924   Josef Stalin becomes leader of Soviet Union after Lenin's death

Communist rebels are still powerful in remote regions of the Philippines.

Which revolution is better?

Many communist regimes came to power by overthrowing democratically-elected governments. But their supporters argue that many democratic countries – notably the United States and France – also gained power through revolution. Is one kind of revolution (leading to a democracy) better than another (which produces a communist government)?

TIMELINE... TIMELINE... TIMELINE... TIMELINE... TIMELINE... TIMELINE...

1927   Stalin expels Leon Trotsky and other rivals from Soviet Communist Party

Power to the people?

Communism means, at its heart, giving power to the people, but what if most of the people are unable to use this power? Maybe they are too poor and badly educated to work in any government. Communist leaders have had to face this problem since the time of Marx. Many outside observers say that they never found a solution to it – and as a result, communism was doomed to failure. Supporters of communism insist that there must be a way of reflecting the people's needs and desires – and they continue to search for one.

MARX, LENIN, MAO AND BEYOND

Karl Marx and his friend Friedrich Engels developed the ideas behind communism as the Industrial Revolution was taking hold in much of Europe. Leaders of other communist countries today try to make those ideas fit – even if their circumstances are very different. Maybe their country is not industrial. Perhaps the population is spread over a huge area. Or maybe the people are familiar with other systems and need to be won over.

In some ways, Marx and Engels were **idealists**; they believed that governments would fade away once people become genuinely communist. Lenin was the first leader to question whether people on their own would ever be able to mount a revolution and then govern themselves – let alone become genuinely communist. The structure of most governments, which work from the top down (for example, general secretary, politburo, party congress and so on) is the result of his thinking.

Mao Zedong (often known as Chairman Mao because of his position in the Chinese Communist Party) introduced a different form of Marxism for two reasons. First, he saw that Marx and Lenin both believed that factory workers and other ordinary people in a country's cities would be the force behind revolution. China then had very little industry, but hundreds of millions of peasant farmers.

Mao believed that these rural people would be at the forefront of the Chinese struggle. He also saw that Marxism-Leninism could easily drift into a form of individual dictatorship, which Mao had witnessed in the Soviet Union under Josef Stalin. **Maoism** called for peasants to be linked to the army – waiting to fight against such elements.

At the height of the Cold War, more than twenty-five countries had communist governments. Most of them operated along Marxist-Leninist or Maoist lines, but one by one they were forced to abandon communism. By the early twenty-first century, that number was down to five – China, Laos, North Korea, Vietnam and Cuba. Each of them, except for North Korea, has had to abandon many elements of Marxism (for example, by allowing small, privately-owned companies to exist) in order to survive.

Vladimir Lenin addresses an eager crowd in 1917, at the height of the Russian Revolution. Lenin's leadership and speaking skills turned many Russians towards communism.

TIMELINE... TIMELINE... TIMELINE... TIMELINE... TIMELINE... TIMELINE...

1934   Mao Zedong leads outlawed Chinese Communist Party on 8,000 km Long March

Different solutions

In 1917, on the eve of the Bolshevik Revolution, only 38 per cent of Russian men and 12 per cent of Russian women could read and write. **Illiteracy** posed a big problem for communist leaders such as Vladimir Lenin. They were struggling to set up a political system that would look after the interests of the masses – in other words, a majority of the Russian population. But if most of these people had no way of choosing between candidates, or of reading laws and regulations, how could they govern themselves?

Lenin came up with a solution that suited his needs, and which became a blueprint for other communist governments. He changed some of the ideas of the communist 'Bible' (the works of Karl Marx) and developed what became known as Marxism-Leninism. Thirty years after the Russian Revolution, Chinese communist leader Mao Zedong came up with another version of communism, which corrected what he saw as mistakes in Lenin's approach (see panel on page 15).

Many political experts believe that the problems with Marxism were far greater than those Lenin and Mao had addressed. One of the biggest was people's personal freedom. Today, as the number of communist governments dwindles, those remaining accept that their people want the freedom to own a car or a house, to travel freely, to read what they like – more than they want the power allotted to them by communism.

A Chinese crowd waves copies of The Little Red Book, *a collection of Mao Zedong's thoughts, in 1967. Mao's influence was enormous, right up to his death in 1976.*

JOSEF STALIN

Josef Stalin had helped Lenin and other communists trigger the Russian Revolution, but he was never seen as Lenin's obvious **successor**. Yet when Lenin died in 1924, Stalin used his position as general secretary to force the Communist Party to turn against his rivals – and to gain overall power himself.

Stalin remained the most powerful person in the Soviet Union until his death in 1953. He ruled as a **dictator**, using secret police and violence to crush any signs of protest or disagreement. He even ordered the murder of Leon Trotsky (who many had wanted to succeed Lenin) in Mexico in 1940.

TIMELINE... TIMELINE... TIMELINE... TIMELINE... TIMELINE... TIMELINE.

1936   Stalin's Great Terror begins: thousands die or disappear; millions sent to prison camps

THE VOTING BOOTH

Communism without the Party?

Russian literacy rates were so low at the start of the twentieth century that it is easy to understand why Vladimir Lenin assumed that the educated leaders of the Communist Party (including himself) knew what the ordinary people wanted and needed in their lives. That, after all, was the reasoning behind the political approach known as Marxism-Leninism.

Do you think that having a highly trained core of people making all the important decisions at the top of the political system is the best way to run a country in the modern era, now far more people can read and write? Could communist systems stick to some of their basic aims if they abandoned the Marxist-Leninist approach?

TIMELINE... TIMELINE... TIMELINE... TIMELINE... TIMELINE... TIMELINE...

1939   Soviet Union signs non-aggression pact with Nazi Germany

The business of government

The slogan 'power to the people' is really tested when communist leaders try to get down to the nitty-gritty of government. How can a communist system build roads, educate people, provide housing or essential supplies when individuals are denied the chance to do these things? The answer is that communist systems have centralized economies. The central planning comes from the leadership, and their orders filter down to every level of government.

Real democracy?

Communist governments have traditionally described themselves as 'democratic'. A true democracy, of course, means rule by the people. That is possible in a small setting – in a club, team or even in a small town – but harder to operate in a whole country. Governments sometimes offer a **referendum** to voters, and the decision made as a result guides law-making on that particular issue.

Most societies accept that it would be impossible to govern along purely democratic lines. Imagine having to vote on every decision that the national government faced – it would be impossible. As a result, voters in Britain, the United States and many other countries elect representatives to act on their behalf. Whether they are Members of Parliament, Congresswomen or Senators, they do their best to reflect public opinion and govern accordingly.

Communist systems also rely on relatively small numbers of people who govern on behalf of everyone, but the voters are not able to

TIMELINE... TIMELINE... TIMELINE... TIMELINE... TIMELINE... TIMELINE

1940	Soviet forces occupy Estonia, Latvia and Lithuania; they become part of Soviet Union
1940	Trotsky murdered in Mexico on orders of Stalin
1941	Germany invades Soviet Union, which joins the Allies against Nazis

Communist Party members assemble for the opening of Cuba's Sixth Communist Party Congress in April 2011.

elect (or vote out) political leaders because communist governments give that power to the Communist Party. The resulting political system works from the top down (see artwork). Politicians rise through the ranks of the Communist Party. Those who reach the highest level enjoy a great deal of power – and are secure from any dissatisfaction that ordinary people might have.

This system allows leaders to make wide-ranging plans without having to worry about disagreements. Many communist projects – dam-building, the space programme, farming policy – follow **five-year plans**. These plans have clear-cut targets to meet by specific deadlines. Sometimes the results of such central planning are astounding: China built the site for the 2008 Olympics in record time. But like a ship that has set off on a wrong course, such huge projects can go horribly wrong if circumstances change along the way.

TIMELINE... TIMELINE... TIMELINE... TIMELINE... TIMELINE... TIMELINE...

1945	Second World War ends. Soviet Union controls eastern Germany and most of eastern Europe
	Unofficial start of the Cold War
1946	Winston Churchill delivers Iron Curtain speech

China's leaders award medals which honour their country's 'outstanding communists' during a ceremony marking the 90th anniversary of China's Communist Party in July 2011.

On page 21 is a chart showing how the Soviet government operated. Most other communist systems adopted similar systems of government along Marxist-Leninist lines.

This classic system of 'top-down' government is also a handy way of understanding how communist political leaders would move in the other direction (towards the top) during their career. The first step for an eager communist politician was always party membership, followed by hard work or crafty dealings to edge past rivals on the way to the top.

TIMELINE... TIMELINE... TIMELINE... TIMELINE... TIMELINE... TIMELINE

1946   Enver Hoxha begins nearly 40 years as communist dictator of Albania

GENERAL SECRETARY

POLITBURO

SECRETARIAT

CENTRAL COMMITTEE

PARTY CONGRESS

GENERAL SECRETARY

The head of the communist government, like a prime minister or president in other systems. The general secretary was elected by members of the central committee.

POLITBURO

The political bureau (shortened to politburo) is a small advisory body similar to the cabinet in other countries. It makes policy (laws) with the general secretary and, like the general secretary, is elected by members of the central committee.

SECRETARIAT

This small group, headed by the general secretary and chosen by the central committee, looked after the organization of the Communist Party and (unlike the politburo) played no part in advising on how to govern the country.

CENTRAL COMMITTEE

This group of about 400 experienced Communist Party members met every six months to recommend policy changes. In some ways, it operated like a Parliament or Congress in other countries in the way it debated laws and government. The central committee members were elected by the party congress.

PARTY CONGRESS

Every five years, about 4,500 Communist Party officials from all over the country met to discuss future policy. The central committee existed to provide day-to-day governing during the long gaps between congresses.

TIMELINE... TIMELINE... TIMELINE... TIMELINE... TIMELINE... TIMELINE...

1947   US announces Truman Doctrine and Marshall Plan to halt communism

Staying in power

A political system can only retain power if it has some way of replacing its leaders when they can no longer govern. Most monarchies are hereditary, so when a monarch dies, the eldest child (often the eldest son) takes the throne. European monarchies have traditionally used the phrase, 'The king is dead; long live the king' to describe this instant transition.

To outsiders, many communist systems seem to treat the handover of power in a similar manner. A leader dies and a successor takes over

| 1948 | Berlin Airlift: UK and US planes cross East Germany to supply cut off West Berlin |
| 1948 | Communist government assumes power in North Korea |

VOICE OF THE PEOPLE

GIVING THANKS
The following letter appears on an official Chinese government website, which has information about the Young Pioneers. Can you imagine such a letter being posted on a website in, for example, Great Britain or Australia?

Dear The motherland:
First I bless you become a new look at the rapid development of science and technology. I am in the fourth grade of the East Beijing Road Primary School. My name is Dong Yixi. When I am a kid, still do not understand the meaning of the Five-star red flag. Until I joined the Young Pioneers, has become a young pioneers, I realized that this red flag not only represents the Chinese, but also make the country safe. Whenever the Five-star red flag rises, I always watch it, national flag in front of a team ritual, to express my deep respect for the flag. In every Monday, I wear on the red scarf, I seem to feel the cries of the revolutionary predecessors, wear on it, I seem to have been the supreme glory. Each school to go home, I remove the red scarf, gently put it on a chair, back into its original place of the treasure with it carefully. As a Chinese Young Pioneers, I respect the Five-star red flag and the red scarf, because they are symbolize my great motherland. I love you, my motherland.

Yours respectfully
Dong Yixi

Young Pioneers wave national flags proudly during celebrations in October 2009, marking the sixtieth anniversary of China's Communist Revolution.

almost immediately. It is hard for outsiders to see how a new leader is chosen – and in some cases, how he or she reached a position from which to assume power. This is because communist leaders are elected by members of the Communist Party, rather than by everyone who lives in the country.

New generations

Systems with elected leaderships have many ways of involving young people in politics, to prepare them to serve their country in elected office later. Children can read newspapers and follow political events on television and on the Internet. Many join groups that promote

TIMELINE... TIMELINE... TIMELINE... TIMELINE... TIMELINE... TIMELINE...

| 1949 | China and more Eastern European countries become communist |
| 1950 | North Korea invades non-communist South Korea; triggers Korean War |

Raul Castro (right) helps his older brother, Fidel, at a meeting of Cuba's Communist Party in April 2011, during which the party passed the leadership from Fidel to his younger brother.

causes such as saving wildlife or combatting world hunger. Through these organizations, young people learn how the political world operates. Some join youth branches of the main political parties, such as Conservative Future, Young Labour and Liberal Youth in Britain.

Communist systems also prepare new generations for leadership. Most of these systems have only one political party – the Communist Party – and their youth branches are there to promote communist attitudes. Most Soviet leaders had their first experience of political life in the Komsomol – a Russian abbreviation for the Young Communist League. China, which still has a communist government, has the

TIMELINE... TIMELINE... TIMELINE... TIMELINE... TIMELINE... TIMELINE.

1953   Korean War ends; communists still control North Korea
        Stalin dies; new Soviet Communist leaders offer more freedom

Too little, too late?

Mikhail Gorbachev introduced reforms in the Soviet Union in the 1980s, hoping that the communist system would be updated and able to continue governing the country. Lenin had been forced to do much the same thing – temporarily – sixty years earlier in order to help the country feed itself (see pages 14-17). China, Vietnam and Cuba have all introduced measures – such as limited private ownership, markets, greater freedom of travel – to help their countries adapt to the changing modern world.

Gorbachev's reforms failed to hold the Soviet Union together. Will economic reforms in other countries spell doom for their communist systems or could they find a way of keeping the best of communism and capitalism?

Mikhail Gorbachev, seen here at a funeral in 2005, was the last leader of the Soviet Union. Despite his efforts to reform the country, the communists lost power and the Soviet Union broke up.

Young Pioneers (for children up to 14) and the Communist Youth League (for those over 14).

For people growing up within a communist system, these youth groups may seem as harmless as boy scouts or girl guides. However, many people living outside the communist world believe that these groups brainwash the younger generation.

TIMELINE... TIMELINE... TIMELINE... TIMELINE... TIMELINE... TIMELINE...

| 1954 | Communists gain power in North Vietnam |
| 1956 | Anti-communist rebellion crushed in Hungary |

Sharing the reins

Traditional Marxists have always been scornful of political elections. They consider them to be nothing more than 'window dressing' which aim to keep capitalists in power (see pages 10–13). Imagine their surprise – and probably shock – to see communists standing for election in some countries. Some countries have communist parties which have gained or shared real power as a result of these elections.

50 AÑOS DE LUCHAS Y VICT

Can it work?

Is there any way that a political philosophy that calls for revolution can survive in societies that cherish free and fair elections? Can communists expect to hold on to power if they win? And would they be prepared to stand down gracefully if they were voted out at an election? Communist parties in several countries have tried to do that in the past; some may continue to do so in the future.

Taking part in free elections means abandoning plans to overthrow existing governments by force (in a revolution). The communist parties in many western European countries decided to do just that in the 1970s. Their new brand of Eurocommunism resembled similar movements in other parts of the world (see below).

A Cuban woman leaves the voting booth during local elections in 2010. Not all candidates had to be Communist Party members, but all were in favour of the party.

EUROCOMMUNISM

Many political observers believe that divisions between the political left and right held some European countries back during the decades after the Second World War. Several European communist parties – especially those in Spain, Italy and Finland – responded by changing their approach.

This new approach, called Eurocommunism, abandoned support for violent revolution and encouraged members to work within the system of each country. They argued that people would choose the path to communism if it were explained sensibly rather than being forced to accept it.

In the 1970s Italy seemed to be on the verge of adopting a system known as a historic **compromise**, which aimed to establish a coalition that included communists and other political parties. This didn't happen, however, because in 1978 terrorists kidnapped and murdered Aldo Moro, the conservative politician who had helped set up the compromise.

TIMELINE... TIMELINE... TIMELINE... TIMELINE... TIMELINE... TIMELINE...

1958   Chinese communists begin Great Leap Forward (brutal high-speed development) to modernize

SALVADOR ALLENDE'S CHILE

The Caribbean island of Cuba adopted a communist government soon after rebel leader Fidel Castro gained power in 1959. The Cuban example inspired other communist rebel movements across **Latin America**, but politicians in Chile took a different approach in 1970. Salvador Allende, a Marxist, won a closely-fought election to become president of the country. Over the next three years he set in place a system he called 'the Chilean path to socialism'. The government took over large companies, increased funding for education and health and generally played a much greater role in people's lives.

Allende made many enemies in doing this, including Chile's army, business people, conservatives and the United States (which feared that Chile would follow the same path as Cuba). After several years of tension, the army staged a coup backed by the US that toppled the government; Allende died during the coup, on 11 September 1973. The new military government punished those who had supported him. Many were forced to flee the country and thousands of others were 'disappeared' by the security forces within Chile and never seen again.

Since the collapse of communism in the Soviet Union and Eastern Europe more than twenty years ago, some of the few remaining communist countries are also rethinking their views on elections. Cuba is typical of this new approach. For decades it has been criticized by western observers, who saw it as a typical communist country with no room for opposition voices.

Cuba's regional elections in April 2010 were an example of this new approach. Voters had the chance to choose candidates who were not representing the Communist Party. And with 95 per cent of Cuban voters taking part in the elections, the government claimed that Cuba was one of the most democratic countries in the world.

TIMELINE... TIMELINE... TIMELINE... TIMELINE... TIMELINE... TIMELINE.

1959   Communist Fidel Castro seizes power in Cuba, 150 km south of US

Italian police recover the body of Aldo Moro, the political leader killed by communist terrorists in 1978.

THE VOTING BOOTH

Can communism work with democracy?

Chile's experiment with an elected Marxist government ended in bloodshed and a military takeover of the government. Italy's historic compromise, which drew the Italian Communist Party into government, ended when terrorists murdered the country's former prime minister, Aldo Moro. Are these events proof that communists will never be able to share power with non-communists in a democracy? Or are they tragic events in the history of those countries – events that might have been even more tragic if communists had remained outside the political system?

TIMELINE... TIMELINE... TIMELINE... TIMELINE... TIMELINE... TIMELINE...

1961   Soviets build **Berlin Wall**, dividing city

Cuba CORREOS 1983 20

X ANIV. CAIDA EN COMBATE DE SALVADOR ALLENDE

A Cuban postage stamp honours Salvador Allende, the Chilean Marxist leader who died in 1973.

VOICE OF THE PEOPLE

TOO SOON TO SUCCEED

Anita (not her real name) is a Chilean who has lived in the UK since Salvador Allende's government was overthrown in 1973. She was a supporter of Allende and felt she had to leave the country after his overthrow because the military government was clamping down on all opposition.

'I was overjoyed when Salvador Allende was elected president. It seemed that we in Chile had not only grown up as a country – being able to conduct a free election – but that Chile was finding a new way forward for other countries. After all, it was still the height of the Cold War. If a country could show how it was able to choose the best bits from East and West, then maybe it would help break down some of the deep divisions that were in place around the world.

Looking back, I can see that it was probably inevitable that Allende's government couldn't last. The mood was too anxious for other elements outside of government – the military, the United States, business leaders – to see that Allende was prepared to work with them, rather than oppose them.

Maybe in another ten or fifteen years, when even the Soviet Union was beginning to change under Gorbachev (see page 25), Allende would have had a chance to survive and succeed. As it was, it was probably too early for that to happen.'

TIMELINE... TIMELINE... TIMELINE... TIMELINE... TIMELINE... TIMELINE.

1962   Cuban Missile Crisis: Soviet Union forced to remove nuclear missiles from Cuba

The wider world

The inscription above Karl Marx's grave in London reads 'Workers of all lands, unite'. Ever since Marx died in 1883, his followers have wondered how to interpret these words. Should they concentrate on setting up communist forms of government in their own country, and set an example for workers in other countries to follow? Or should they try to light the spark of revolution in every country?

The ideas behind Eurocommunism, the brief presidency of Salvador Allende (see page 28) and the 2008 general election triumph of a Maoist political party in Nepal show that many communists are happy to concentrate on their own country. But over the years, powerful

(see page 28)

TIMELINE... T~~IMELIN~~... . TIMELINE... TIMELINE.. ~~TIMELIN~~E... TIMELINE...

| 1964 | US joins Vietnam conflict between communist north and non-communist south |

communist states such as the Soviet Union and China have reached out to communists in other countries. Some communist aid was linked to the Cold War (see panel below): the Soviet Union supplied money and weapons to North Korea, Egypt, Ethiopia, Cuba and other countries that considered adopting communism. Cuba even sent troops to help communist rebels in Angola and Mozambique.

But the small countries that were the focus of communist (and western anti-communist) aid sometimes played the big powers off against each other. Egypt and Cambodia are two examples, turning first to one of the big powers and then to its rival in order to get valuable aid. The benefits of being 'paid twice' were enormous – but so were the risks.

THE COLD WAR

During the Second World War, the world's two most powerful countries, the United States and the Soviet Union, fought together against Hitler's forces. But soon after the war ended, these two superpowers began to view each other with suspicion. The United States feared that the Soviet Union was trying to spread communism across the world – and even into the United States itself. Meanwhile the Soviet Union (which had suffered far more in the war) was desperate to protect its borders.

The Soviet Union put pressure on many east European countries to become communist during the late 1940s. This was partly to spread communism and partly to protect the Soviet Union from another military invasion. The United States responded by helping western European countries rebuild their economies, at the same time strengthening them against threats from eastern Europe and the Soviet Union.

Battlelines were being drawn in what became known as the Cold War between the superpowers and their supporters. During the next four decades, each side tried to score against the other. The superpowers didn't fight each other directly, but supported their allies against the other side in regional conflicts. These Cold War conflicts were localized, but people around the world feared that they might escalate and draw the two superpowers into another world war.

The Cold War lasted until 1991, when the Soviet Union ceased to exist as a country and Russia abandoned communism.

TIMELINE... TIMELINE... TIMELINE... TIMELINE... TIMELINE... TIMELINE.

1968   Soviet troops invade Czechoslovakia to crush anti-communists

VOICE OF THE PEOPLE

THE IRON CURTAIN

Winston Churchill, who was the British prime minister during the Second World War, addressed students at Westminster College, Missouri, in March 1946. He spoke of his concerns for Europe. Having freed the continent from the threat of Hitler, Europeans faced another menace, in Churchill's opinion. He was concerned and saddened by the way that one of the wartime Allies, the Soviet Union, was gaining so much control over eastern Europe. The phrase he used to describe Europe's post-war dividing line – an 'iron curtain' – captured people's imaginations.

'A shadow has fallen upon the scenes so lately lighted by the Allied victory. Nobody knows what Soviet Russia and its communist international organization intends to do in the immediate future, or what are the limits, if any, to their expansive and **proselytizing** tendencies... From Stettin in the Baltic to Trieste in the Adriatic an iron curtain has descended across the Continent. Behind that line lie all the capitals of the ancient states of central and eastern Europe. Warsaw, Berlin, Prague, Vienna, Budapest, Belgrade, Bucharest and Sofia, all these famous cities and the populations around them lie in what I must call the Soviet sphere, and all are subject in one form or another, not only to Soviet influence but to a very high and, in some cases, increasing measure of control from Moscow.'

Winston Churchill gives his famous 'iron curtain' speech in 1946.

TIMELINE... TIMELINE... TIMELINE... TIMELINE... TIMELINE... TIMELINE...

1970   Salvador Allende elected president of Chile leading coalition including communists

KEY DATES IN THE COLD WAR

1945	Second World War ends; Soviet Union controls eastern Germany and most of eastern Europe. Unofficial start of Cold War
1947	US announces Truman Doctrine and Marshall Plan to halt advance of communism
1948	Communist government takes power in North Korea
1949	China and more eastern European countries become communist
1950	North Korea invades non-communist South Korea, triggering Korean War
1953	Stalin dies; new Soviet Communist leaders offer more freedom
1954	Communists gain power in North Vietnam
1956	Anti-communist rebellion crushed in Hungary
1959	Communist Fidel Castro seizes power in Cuba
1961	Soviets build Berlin Wall
1962	Soviet Union forced to remove nuclear missiles from Cuba
1964	US enters Vietnam conflict
1968	Soviet troops invade Czechoslovakia to crush anti-communists
1970	Salvador Allende elected president of Chile
1973	Allende dies as Chile's military leaders seize power
1975	US troops leave Vietnam as communist North captures southern capital
1975	Cambodia's communist government kills up to 2 million
1977	Angola and Mozambique adopt communist governments
1979	Soviet Union invades Afghanistan to protect pro-communist government
1979	Pro-communist Sandinista rebels gain control of Nicaragua
1985	Mikhail Gorbachev becomes Soviet leader; begins reform
1989	Berlin Wall falls; most east European countries abandon communism
1991	Gorbachev resigns; Soviet Union ceases to exist. Cold War is over.

Communism and the media

One of the cherished freedoms in countries such as Britain, Australia, the United States and France is the **free press**. This term goes beyond describing material produced on printing presses and refers to the flow of information, as well as how freely individuals can receive it, whether via mobile phones, television and radio, emails or the Internet.

All these forms of communication are known as the media. People in countries with a free press expect to be able to receive information without government interference or censorship. Free reporting of news events – plus occasional criticism of the government – helps voters decide whether to re-elect their political leaders or to vote them out at the next election.

Party control

Communist governments take a different view. A ruling Communist Party outlaws rival political parties and exercises strict control over the media. The party decides what can be printed in newspapers, broadcast on television and radio and how much of the Internet the people can reach. (The Chinese Communist Party, for example, blocks many websites and search engines.)

How can a government justify such behaviour? The answer is similar to the reason political opposition is stifled: the government believes that an uncontrolled flow of information is bad for people. What some see as unlimited choice – of products to buy, services to receive, things to read – communist governments see as rich companies and individuals (capitalists) working together to keep the people in their place.

TIMELINE... TIMELINE... TIMELINE... TIMELINE... TIMELINE... TIMELINE...

1973   Allende dies as Chile's military leaders seize power

Even the strictest communists probably realize that they are fighting a losing battle because information slips into the country despite restrictions. But they also fear that having tasted freedom, people will demand more… and will eventually get rid of communism. That is understandable as most communist governments collapsed in the late 1980s because their citizens wanted a different way of life.

Presenting an image

On one level, it seems easy for communist leaders and governments to decide what not to broadcast. But in the twenty-first century, people expect to see television images and to listen to their radios – regardless of their country's political system. To address this

Fidel Castro visited the US in April 1959, less than four months after his rebel forces overthrew Cuban dictator Fulgencio Batista. The US government correctly suspected that Castro would form a communist government, but the American media loved his rebel image and tales of jungle combat.

TIMELINE... TIMELINE... TIMELINE... TIMELINE... TIMELINE... TIMELINE.

1975   US troops leave Vietnam; forces from communist north capture southern capital

VOICE OF THE PEOPLE

Whistling the wrong music
Marlies Steiner was only fifteen when the Berlin Wall was demolished and her native city was reunited. More than twenty years later, she still has vivid memories about living under the communist system in East Berlin.

'Because we were so close to West Berlin, we knew more about the outside world than people in other parts of East Germany did. We could see the big cars and brighter clothing that the people in the West had – plus we knew of people who had managed to get across to the other side.

There were many sad and scary stories – families that were divided, people being shot and killed as they tried to get across. But looking back, I can almost see the funny side of this division. For example, a man who worked with my father was called into his boss's office. The boss was furious, accusing the man of spreading anti-communist propaganda. Despite the man's denials, the boss continued angrily, saying that several fellow employees could provide **testimony.**

It turned out that those other workers had heard the man whistling the theme music to Bonanza, an American television programme about cowboys. And the only way that the man could have known that music was to have aimed his television aerial at the West, which was forbidden. But we asked ourselves – how did the others know what the music was if they hadn't done the same thing?'

problem, communist governments seem to go back to the days of ancient Rome when rulers thought that if people had enough to eat and decent entertainment, they would be content and easier to govern. Communist governments make sure that their citizens have enough food even if it is never very varied. The entertainment comes in the form of stirring musical performances, action films and lots of sporting events.

Many of the films and TV programmes in today's China – or in the final years of the Soviet Union – would have seemed daring in the 1950s, when every story had to deal directly with communist themes. But with the exception of North Korea (which has successfully sealed itself off from the outside world for decades), communist countries have moved away from outright **propaganda**.

TIMELINE... TIMELINE... TIMELINE... TIMELINE... TIMELINE... TIMELINE...

1975   Cambodia's Khmer Rouge (communist) government kills up to 2 million

Several generations of a Chinese family crowd around a television to watch celebrations marking the sixtieth anniversary of communist rule in China.

SCREEN VERSIONS

Throughout the Cold War, communist and non-communist governments used propaganda to influence opinions about world politics. Communist films and television programmes often showed evil factory owners and businessmen controlling America and other capitalist countries. They focused on the awful living conditions and illness of poor people in those countries. Meanwhile, they showed people in the Soviet Union and other communist countries smiling and singing as they worked on farms or in factories.

At the same time, many people in the West feared that communists (known as Reds) were secretly gaining influence – and that they would end the freedoms that Americans and others enjoyed. The titles of some films from the late 1940s and early 1950s reflect those fears: *Red Planet Mars*, *I Married a Communist* and *The Red Menace*.

More recent films have portrayed the fall of communism in Europe, sometimes comically. The German film *Goodbye, Lenin!* tells of a loyal East German communist who has a heart attack. When she wakes up, the East German communist government has fallen and Germany is about to be reunited as a capitalist country. The woman's children know that this news will come as a shock to their mother, so they behave as if they still lived in a communist country.

TIMELINE... TIMELINE... TIMELINE... TIMELINE... TIMELINE... TIMELINE.

1977   Angola and Mozambique adopt communist governments after wars of independence

Where did it go wrong?

Imagine turning on the TV to find just one – or maybe two – channels broadcasting political speeches and perhaps an opera about a cement factory. Or queuing for an hour to buy oranges, then being allowed to buy just three. Or going to buy a new shirt and finding that there were four in your size – but they were all grey.

This is partly an exaggeration of what daily life in a communist country was like. There were times when shops had better selections of goods, but also times when people have struggled to feed or clothe their families (especially in extreme communist countries such as North Korea).

Shoppers in Warsaw form a lengthy queue outside a butcher's shop in August 1980. Constant food shortages prompted anti-communist protests later that year, which had swept communism away in Poland and all eastern Europe by 1990.

TIMELINE... TIMELINE... TIMELINE... TIMELINE... TIMELINE... TIMELINE...

1979   Soviet Union invades Afghanistan to protect pro-communist government

A Formula 1 racing car drives through Red Square in the heart of Moscow, in 2008. It would be impossible to imagine a more fitting symbol of capitalism succeeding in what was once the heart of international communism.

Workers' paradise or nightmare?

This seems a far cry from the workers' paradises that communist leaders promised. As citizens of those countries learned more about life outside the communist world (see pages 35–38), the public mood has often become angry. Beginning with Poland in 1980, the communist governments of eastern Europe faced protests – these were often illegal but they grew by the year.

By the end of that decade, the Berlin Wall (a symbol of communist harshness) had fallen, and most of the countries behind the Iron Curtain had rid themselves of communist rule. The protests even reached the two largest communist countries. The Chinese army crushed a massive pro-democracy protest in the capital, Beijing, in 1989. The Soviet Union fared even worse; it unravelled in 1991 and the new Russian government began dismantling the communist system.

How did all this happen? Some observers say that it is human nature to want the individual freedoms that communist systems stifle.

TIMELINE... TIMELINE... TIMELINE... TIMELINE... TIMELINE... TIMELINE.

1979   Pro-communist Sandinista rebels gain control of Nicaragua

> **VOICE OF THE PEOPLE**

HUMAN NATURE?

Sasha has lived in Kiev, capital of Ukraine, all his fifty-six years. He describes himself as a product of the communist system (Ukraine was part of the Soviet Union), but prefers living in Ukraine's current democracy.

'In many ways, the political system is less important than human nature. After all, I think that people will be selfish, or kind, or funny – or whatever – whether they're in a communist system, or capitalist. Take me, for example. I'm the sort of person who knows where to find a good bargain. When we lived under communism, of course, there were no such things as bargains: you just bought what was available at the shops.

But my friends and I were members of Komsomol (the Young Communist League – like a communist version of the Scouts). In fact, I was in charge of propaganda for our group. Each month we would receive money to be used for propaganda purposes. Instead, we used it to buy records and speakers so that we could have discos. So in that way, we could still have our fun and not be concerned about the political system.

Not everyone was so comfortable with communism, though. My grandmother had three apple trees by her cottage. Each year she would share her apples with her neighbours and turn the surplus into a few bottles of cider, which she would sell. That is, until the police came round and accused her of being a capitalist. They threatened to cut the trees down if they caught her selling any cider ever again. She lived in fear after that.

I think that the big system of communism failed because it didn't understand human nature. Of course, people like my granny want a little reward for their hard work. To call her some sort of criminal made everyone wonder whether they wanted all that "equality" after all.'

Communism, at its heart, is an economic and not a political theory. It believes that the state (organized politics in a country) will wither away once the people become happy with their lives. Instead, it seems that communist states have withered away, replaced in most countries by some form of capitalist democracy.

TIMELINE... TIMELINE... TIMELINE... TIMELINE... TIMELINE... TIMELINE...

1980 Solidarity, an independent trade union, is formed in Poland

Have Coca-Cola, MP3 players and pizza achieved what decades of Cold War tension failed to do – and toppled communism? Or can the remaining communist countries adapt to these threats?

In late 1989, delighted Germans helped to destroy the Berlin Wall, one of the most hated symbols of the communist era.

THE VOTING BOOTH

The party's over
Can you think of any way in which communist governments can thrive in the age of modern communications? Or is the communist system simply evil and outdated, as its enemies claim?

Looking ahead

As the communist governments of Europe toppled one by one in the late 1980s and early 1990s, many people predicted that communism itself would be finished by the beginning of the twenty-first century. One American political observer, Francis Fukuyama, described that period as 'the end of history'. In his view, the great conflicts that had defined history – rich versus poor, city versus country, capitalism versus Marxism – had all been resolved. Capitalism had beaten communism and people had no more need to protest because they could buy and sell as they pleased.

Fukuyama's prediction now seems out of date, and as wildly optimistic as Marx's prediction that history and politics would end with everyone living in a communist workers' paradise. Five countries, including the world's largest, stubbornly cling to communism. Will they decide that enough is enough, or will they find a way forward that retains the best elements of communism as well as capitalism?

Mixing things up

Many countries that were eager to get rid of communism – especially the Soviet Union – turned to a form of capitalism that kept some of the worst features of the old system. For example, Russia's vast energy reserves, once controlled by the government, were sold to individuals who had links with former communist officials. The income from the oil and gas fields went not to the government, but to the new private owners. Some of them are now among the richest people in the world… but ordinary Russians have not benefitted.

So some apparently capitalist democracies are capable of adopting some of the worst features of communism – putting power and

TIMELINE… TIMELINE… TIMELINE… TIMELINE… TIMELINE… TIMELINE…

1989   Berlin Wall falls; most eastern European countries abandon communism

money in the hands of a few who are outside public control. Wealthy individuals who own national newspapers and television networks, for example, can control the flow of information almost as easily as communist governments. Since 2010, Britain has seen a series of scandals relating to the way in which one such large company operated.

Similar accusations have been made against some of the companies linked to the world of computers and the Internet. One company has sent trucks with cameras to towns and cities in many countries, and put those images up for all to see. Some observers object strongly to such behaviour, comparing it with the way in which communist governments used spies to check up on people.

VOICE OF THE PEOPLE

CUBA'S YOUTH

For many years, Cuba was one of the most strictly controlled communist countries. Planning was centralized and people had few personal freedoms. In the last two decades, its government has loosened its strict control, allowing people more freedom – especially the freedom to set up small private businesses.

One example of the 'new Cuba' is the website www.havanatimes.org. The site offers people from within Cuba and beyond the chance to discuss politics openly, even if some Cubans themselves are still worried about being punished for criticizing the government. Recently the site posed the question, 'Is the Future of Cuba's Revolution Truly Guaranteed?' Many people responded, some predicting the end of communism and others trying to help Cuba find a way of making the best of communism work. The comment below (from Friedrich) is typical of many who look to Cuba's youth for a way forward.

*'A conflict of generations (the old ones don't understand the youngsters and vice versa) is not only a problem of capitalist countries. Give more strength to the youth and listen to the wisdom of the elderly would be an ideal combination, as well as open up more room for private **initiatives**. If someone doesn't feel well, you have to ask why, the same thing with the youngsters. The leading people should listen to their voices, involve them more, and once [it becomes] motivated more, I don't see why socialism should end with the older generation.'*

TIMELINE... TIMELINE... TIMELINE... TIMELINE... TIMELINE... TIMELINE.

1989   Pro-democracy protests crushed in Beijing

At the same time, most remaining communist governments have loosened their control over their economies. The result is that individuals are now setting up private businesses in China, Vietnam and Cuba. The communist governments have decided that some economic freedoms – as well as social freedoms – might be the best way of preserving their form of government.

Will these concessions be enough to keep communist governments in power? Perhaps they will, and people in capitalist countries who have been hurt by the **credit crunch** will look to those countries for guidance. It would have been hard, during the tense years of the Cold War, for communists to accept that the west had some better ideas, and vice-versa. Perhaps now that the Cold War is over, individuals and governments might be able to find a way to pick and choose the best ideas from the two systems that once seemed so divided. Only time will tell.

A Russian woman holds a communist poster during a May Day celebration in Moscow, nineteen years after the fall of the communist government. Some Russians dislike the confusion and crime in their new society, and they look back to the security of life under communism.

TIMELINE... TIMELINE... TIMELINE... TIMELINE... TIMELINE... TIMELINE...

1991   Gorbachev resigns and Soviet Union ceases to exist. Most experts agree that Cold War is over

Glossary

Aristotle   A Greek philosopher (383–322 BCE) whose writing still influences modern thinkers.

Berlin Wall   A heavily defended barrier that the communist East German government built in 1961 to stop its citizens from crossing into non-communist West Germany.

bourgeois   A term used as an insult by communists which describes a social class that is most concerned with making and holding on to money.

class   People who are grouped together according to their position in society or wealth.

coalition   An alliance of groups (such as political parties) which agree to work together for a specific purpose.

Cold War   A period of tense political conflict (but never outright war) between the Soviet Union and the United States lasting from 1945 to 1991.

compromise   A way of settling a dispute in which each side gives in a little to the other.

comrade   A friendly word used by a communist to describe another communist.

credit crunch   A time of international economic hardship beginning in 2008 when many banks had difficulty with their borrowing and lending (credit).

damask   A heavy, patterned silk or linen fabric.

democracy   A system of government in which people choose their political leaders by voting.

deposed   Removed from power, often by force.

dictator   A ruler with total power over a country.

empire   A group of separate nations ruled by a single political leader.

five-year plan   A long-term plan for industry or farming, used by communist governments.

free press   The freedom to write (or present on television or radio) whatever one wants, unless those opinions are harmful to others in the country.

Goethe   Johann Wolfgang von Goethe (1749–1832) was a German writer, artist and scientist who was seen as one of the greatest minds of his time.

idealist   Someone who remains hopeful of the best outcome.

illiteracy   Being unable to read and write.

initiative   An organized project.

Latin America   An area covering most of South America and parts of North America and the Caribbean region that has a historical connection with Spain or Portugal.

mandate   The right (of a political leader or government) to follow a particular policy because the voters chose their party and policies.

Maoism   A form of Marxist political thought that believes in constant revolution by linking peasants with the army.

Marxism   The political theories of Karl Marx, centring on class struggle and forming the basis of communism.

peasant   A poor farmer.

propaganda   The spreading of news, rumour and sometimes lies to gain political support or to hurt the reputation of those who oppose you.

proselytizing   Trying to convert others to a belief or opinion.

provisional government   The emergency (provisional) government in Russia that lasted eight months from the resignation of Tsar Nicholas II in March 1917 until the Bolshevik (Communist) Revolution.

referendum   A special vote, usually on a single issue, that all voters decide.

regime   Describes a form of government; the term is often used as an insult.

republic   A form of government in which voters choose representatives to govern.

Second World War   The war which began in Europe but spread around the world between 1939 and 1945.

serf   A poor farmer who works on a landowner's property.

Soviet Union   A communist country, including Russia and 14 other areas, which lasted from 1917 to 1991.

successor   Someone who succeeds (takes over from) another person in power.

testimony   An official recollection of an event by someone who was present.

tsar   The ruler of the Russian Empire.

western   A term used to describe countries or systems of thought that are not communist.

Books

The Collapse of Communism (Witness to History)   R. Stewart (Heinemann Library, 2004)

Under a Red Sky: Memoir of a Childhood in Communist Romania   Haya Leah Molnar (Farrar Straus Giroux, 2010)

Understanding the Communist Manifesto (Words that Changed the World)   D. Boyle (Rosen, 2010)

Websites

China Today
www.chinatoday.org

Havana Times
www.havanatimes.org

UNICEF Voices of Youth
www.voicesofyouth.org/en/sections/

United Nations Cyberschoolbus
cyberschoolbus.un.org/

Index